Angela's
footsteps...

*To Jane
with love from
Angela
02/04/18*

🦶 by Angela Cobbin-Owen

Angela Owen

Published privately in the United Kingdom in 2018

Copyright © 2018 Angela Cobbin-Owen

Design Ginny Wood | gin.wood@sky.com
Illustrations Alodie Fielding | thecrookedstyle.com

ISBN paperback 978-1-5272-2193-2

All rights reserved.
No part of this publication may be reproduced
in any form or by any means without the written
permission of the publisher.

The moral right of Angela Cobbin-Owen
to be identified as the author of this work
has been asserted in accordance
with the Copyright, Design and Patents Act 1988.

Acknowledgements

My thanks go to Ginny Wood,
Graphic Designer for her unwavering
support in the production of this book
of poems and Illustrator Alodie Fielding's
wonderfully interpreted drawings.

And last but not least, a big thank you to
my husband for all his encouragement.

Dedication

For all the good years

Darling!

I'm not naming names but she's fairly well known
All I will say is some call her Joan.
It's really quite tragic
I'm thinking of late when
Her views on some play
To me plainly she'd state
Most critical clearly
Without supposition
None of it good but in her position
She felt it unwise to hold views of which
If heard by the others they'd call her a bitch.

Circa 1900

In one moment I captured
That look in her eyes
Days of her youth
Dress well below thighs
Hours of embroidery
School with a Tutor
Afternoon teas
With a well chosen suitor
And our generation
What does she care
Hippies and drugs
Men with long hair
Her knowledge of freedom
Like this was quite spare
And thinking such things
For her would be rare
Days were more gentle
But was it much fun
Well whatever it was
It's all been undone.

Her

I've remembered that woman
She sat on the wall
With her children, and smoking
They were all very small
Where is she now
In her ill-fitting dress
No stockings, just slippers
Her hair a birds nest.
Well, while I've been writing
I'm sorry to say
Right out of the blue
She's back there today.

Party

Crowded room

Noisy rabble

Beckoning smiles

And so we dabble

In flowery speeches

Tittle tattle

Inhaling fumes

Of cloudy air

See drunken eyes

With vacant stare

Insipid voice

That tries in vain but

Cannot state their views

Too plain

Make excuse, leave

So much fun

Then ask ourselves

Why did we come.

Read the papers
Hear the news
Your party's in
You like their views
They cash the chips
And clear the table
Call the tunes
Through you they're able
They bleed us dry
The parties squabble
Through turbulent years
The scales they wobble
The end is nigh
On you they dote
But fickle you
You've changed your vote.

Fog

It draped its swirl

Beneath the trees

Their darkened shadows

Shaped to freeze as each

Drop of worn out rain

Stains the ground within the lane

And there beneath

Leaf weighted crowd

The mist has draped

Its icy shroud.

Pause

If we think for a moment

Where we're going

What we are doing

Right this minute

To and fro-ing

Some will ride the waves

Of sorrow

Some have laughter

Each tomorrow.

The Orator

His words were clear
And yet they fell
Upon the air as tho' a spell
Had deafened all
Without a sign to
The poet's magic rhyme

Around the room
A fashioned horde
With others shared expressions bored
Afraid of life
The voice of time
The poet's magic rhyme

With tired gaze
Undaunted still
He tried in vain
Their hearts to fill
With beauty so sublime
This poet's magic rhyme.

Behind the brightness
Of her eyes
The hooded veil
Hides all her sighs.

A half forgotten moment

Trying to catch those fleeting glimpses
Remembering
Touching your face in the photograph
It's the garden where you're seen
You're not there now
Or are you where
You set that lovely scene
Bring me the last rose of summer.

A Day Out

We passed the brooding mountains
Grey but for the want of rain
Tears stung the back of my eyes
A moment in memory lane.

The rain then plagued us all the way
Towards our destination
Fish and chips, Portmeirion and
Blaenau-Ffestiniog station.

We were having a great day out
But for the want of some sun
In spite of a puncture, umbrellas the damp
We agreed on the whole
It was fun.

Bonds

Where are my friends
When I want to chat
Of this and that
Sometimes not there
But when the chips are down
They come out of thin air
Doing their bit
Seeing one through
It's hard on them most when
It's hardest for you
I think of them now
And if some day
Their lives are laid bare
No matter the time
Or distance and age...

I'll be there.

Time wasting

It was one of those days

You'll know them I think

The typewriter bless it had gone on the blink

It finally coughed up a misprint and sighed

There was too much to write

So it curled up and died

With flourish of pen

There was naught else to do

I managed to scribble the day away too.

There was a tree both tall and gracious
Who's rich green leaves dressed arms so spacious
Where once was life has now been cleft
And broken stump is all that's left.

Into the truck with heavy thump

An ignominious end

The careless throwing of that final stump

Defeated

Now in sad submission

Such fearless noble Knight

Left dying in the winter

On a cold raw night.

Miffed

I'd like you to be more aware

Before you wander off to stare

At that lovely figure

So young

And full of vigour

Tossing her fair hair

This way and that

Leaving me sitting

Like some old hat.

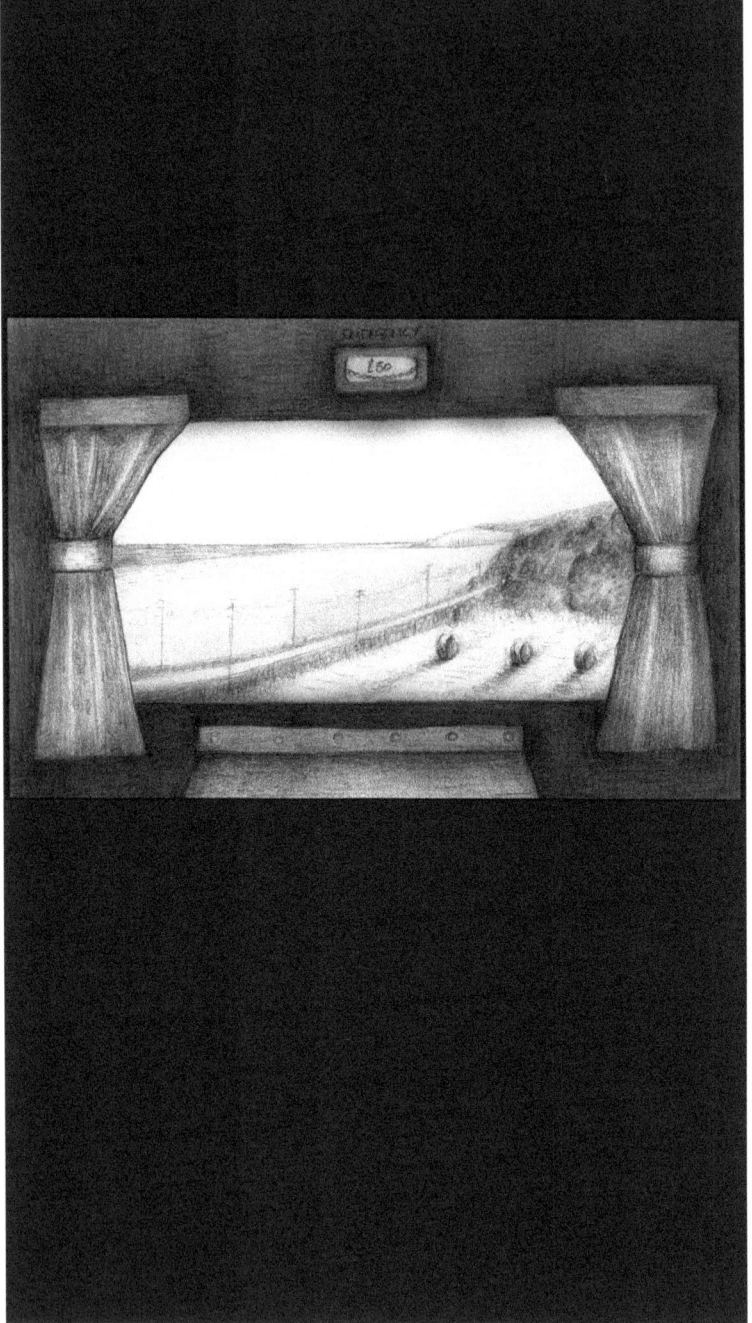

Daydreaming

I'm aware that he's talking to me

But I'm only half listening for

There is the sea

Beyond the long road

Miles away still

Narrow and winding

Its way up the hill

Why can't he see

I'm enthralled with the view

The countryside coloured

In every hue

The ploughed fields rich brown

Yellow and red

Why can't he see

What I'm seeing instead.

The poets write of loving couples

Romeo and Juliet

Abelard and Heloise

Forever gone...

Yet still live on.

Procession

Follow the flowers the bright coloured flowers

Passing through the town

Remembering the hours

With a sprinkling of people

Oblivious

Save one or two

Who

Standing still on that sky blue day

Watched us driving so slowly

Away

Along the front

On a road to forever

Wishing somehow it could never

Be this day

This final journey

On a February clear

By a calm blue sea

Margaret Elizabeth

Comes down the aisle

Goodbye

Farewell a while.

War

It must have been a sight to see
A ship coming home from the war
People waving
Crowding the quayside
Cheering the men as they came ashore

It must have been a joy to behold
A son coming home from the fight
Among the crowd
Surrounding them all
Laughing crying holding him tight

It must have been a terrible time
For the one who stood as a stone
Seeing the prayer
On her unmoving lips
Turning away quite alone

It must have been a sight to see
The stuff from which heroes are made
Hearing the stories one year to the next
Growing in stature as memories fade.

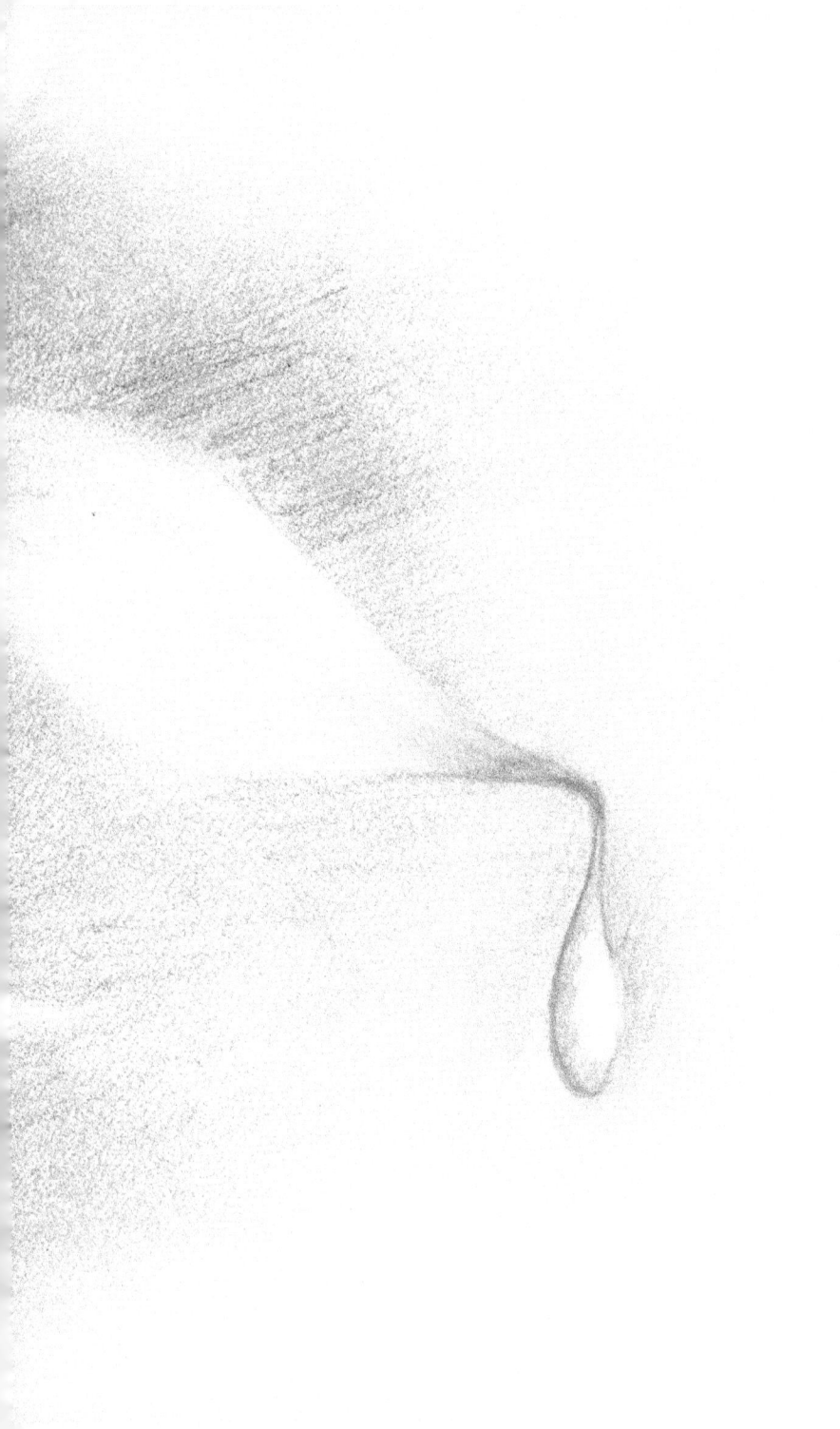

How Still

How still the day, the air

Slowing down

Just the ticking of the clock

Taking time away

Yet ticks on in hope

Some miracle

Keeping your familiar face

Your laughter

The all-embracing nearness

Of you, still here

No fanfare

No fond farewell

Awaiting that moment, when

It comes unexpectedly

Uninvited

And your precious light

Goes out on a summers day

In a far off other place

I am crying but

My eyes are dry.

Pit Stop

Deep in that dark place
From the coal face
They've fetched
The blackest of dust
In their veins
It's now etched.

Life

A single pebble
Thrown to the sea
Leaving slight ripple

Like you and me.

In memory of Jane

Passing Romance

The shine was wearing thin
He could tell
What once had been exciting
Now was... well...
Let's say... losing colour
Fewer were the calls
Between one another
She's met someone else
Well two can play that game
Even though he fancied her
What a shame.

Tears like rain flow down a faceless window

It is the dawn of love

That pure as dew

In the morning sun

It burns away.

Procrastination

I'll telephone or you'll call me ...
No... I'll call you... We always do.
Next week... next month... when? It could be ages
Before we meet again. Well, let's leave it a bit
Then... You'll call me or I'll call you...
We always do.

A walk in the autumn
Down country lanes
Crumbling the leaves
From around their veins
Trampling them underfoot
Golden and browned
Loving their crispness
That crunching sound
Feeling the rainfall
Sharp on the face
Enormous tear-drops
Like clear spreading lace
Washing them down
Upon the ground
Once crackling, now soft
And slushing around.

Lady Jane

Sandy coloured
Runs away
Brings back a bone
Another day
She'd chase the dogs
Across the park
Sleep in the kitchen
When it was dark
Summer walks
Romps in the snow
And from our home
Sometimes she'd go

I took her once
Down to the sea
The only time
She ran from me
In our garden
Where she now lies
I often gazed
Recalled I'd cried
When I found one morning
My friend had died.

Sunny Day

A picture of a happy day in April
What were we laughing about in the garden
With slope and stream
And oaks so old.

I often dream
About that special day
We laughed talked and puffed our way
Up the carpet of grass
So soft to tread
My mother's hair now white
Once red.

I was watching Miss World

In considerable pain

I hadn't been well

I ought to explain

What with wear and with tear

Not to mention my hair

I was feeling

Decidedly plain.

If I die, I'll lay me down
To sleep in my bed
Or, will I stepping on a bus perhaps
Cause some concern and fuss
Collapsing on the boarding stage
Whilst others scrambling over me
In awful rush hour rage
Imagine I've been drinking
What am I thinking
Perhaps I'll be out walking or
Talking to a friend when
My life comes to an end but
No, I'll lay me down to sleep
In my bed
Or will I.

Lightning Source UK Ltd.
Milton Keynes UK
UKHW02f0306140318
319410UK00002B/10/P